MADAME ECOSSE

Madame Ecosse

MARION McCREADY

 EYEWEAR PUBLISHING

First published in 2017
by Eyewear Publishing Ltd
Suite 333, 19-21 Crawford Street
Marylebone, London W1H 1PJ
United Kingdom

Cover design and typeset by Edwin Smet
Author photograph by Jamie McCready
Cover artwork 'Out of the Night a Shadow Passed',
by Hannah Frank 1908-2008. © The Estate of Hannah Frank,
used by permission of the estate.

Printed in England by TJ International Ltd, Padstow, Cornwall

ISBN 978-1-911335-21-4

*Eyewear wishes to thank Jonathan Wonham for his
generous patronage of our press.*

WWW.EYEWEARPUBLISHING.COM

to Jamie
shadow tracker and soulmate

and to Sorley and Ruby

Marion McCready
was born in Stornoway and lives in
Dunoon, Argyll, Scotland. She studied Politics,
Classics and Philosophy at Glasgow University.
Her poems have been published widely,
including in *Poetry*, *Edinburgh Review*, *The
Glasgow Herald* and *Be The First To Like This:
New Scottish Poetry*. She won a Scottish Book
Trust New Writers Award in 2013. Her first
full-length collection, *Tree Language*, was
published by Eyewear in 2014, chosen
by Jon Stone as the Melita Hume
poetry prize winner.

TABLE OF CONTENTS

REDWOOD AVENUE I:
WOMEN OF THE AVENUE

Whoever comes to this garden
must enter through me

and my forty-eight sisters.
Our thunder-roots meet

under a grass sea.
Our brittle limbs rise,

catching fog, learning
survival day by day.

ROSE HIPS AND THISTLES

It's been a long Indian summer
and the hips are rotting on the beach rose.

I can almost taste their sour skins —
red balls of seeds glistening

like fiery cauldrons in the late September sun;
green tentacles dripping below.

I'm dreaming of exotic gentians,
alpines, delphiniums.

But it's the last of the flowering thistles
that stand before me

with their decadent helmets and feathers.
I think of Ellen Willmott

secretly scattering thistle seeds
in her neighbours' gardens,

spreading pieces of herself — a legacy, to grow
and grow again when her body

is lowered to feed the earth
in a last great act of love.

SELFIE

And now shall I strike a new pose?
And now? – The bunting,
the furious triangles at my back.

With your thumb you swipe past me.
You may hide, you may block me
but I travel at the speed of light.

I'm in your pocket, your bag,
every screen in your home
projects me.

Every day I transform –
today I am a funnel-web spider
with bright red fangs.

I rush out of my silken lair, legs
raised, glistening venom.
Every photo racier than the last –

What do you think of this?
Now I am a barn owl – I shriek, I hunger,
I will tear you apart.

I creep out of my tree hole,
undulate through dark matter.
You can't help but touch my heart

-shaped face
or slide into the black fruit of my eyes.
I fly silently through the air,

I quarter the ground.
Now I am here, now
I am here, my smile bare

and infinitely travelling towards you
there and there.

DEATH OF A TULIP

Dutch tulip,
little red Dutch tulip with your black-blooded interior
exposed, flattened. Curling at the edges –
your feather-petals like a dried up vital organ.

You old wine stain, six-fingered,
reaching beyond yourself. You smell of mud.

In your exposed heart you hide many deaths –
in your black circle
you are a city in mourning.

A throat slit open,
your yellows are venom.
Oh tulip, tulipe, tulipa!

You're a piece of cake – fingered but not eaten.
You're a piece of spoiled ham
with pig trotter petals and a black snout.

I remember when your tightly clenched mouth
first opened – it was as if Christmas had come early;
or like when the angry wound up ball of a baby
smiled for the first time.

You bloomed like a penitent soul
under the gaze of our Father.

It was then I hated you, tulip.
Pure McIntosh, skin the colour of communion;
soaking up the air, drawing everyone in.

All I could see was you,
red head against the window.

But now you drip more soggy orange than red
all over my sink, breathing your last breath.

Consider the tulip.

TWILIGHT SLEEP

I.

Its tiny hands, curling like feather sticks,
wave above the cot.
It seems to know me.

My baby appeared suddenly
the way a toadstool appears overnight
in a garden. My little puffball,

my stinkhorn and witch's egg,
my death cap.
My destroying angel

has a toadstool head.
They took him from me. For three days
I lay in this damp bed –

the Firth of Clyde stretching before me
in all its medical glitter.
Somehow I lost my shoes.

Barefoot, I ran across motorways,
ran up the grassy hill, Tony calling
on the phone. I didn't answer.

I can't remember the last time I peed.
Nightly I'm giving birth
though the baby never comes.

And the wooden doll beside me
grows woodier by the day.

II.

Honey, could you open the suitcase
and get me my head?

I woke with a sharp pain —
they injected me.
   I woke the next morning —
they brought me my baby.

I am flat and light as the horizon.
Where did the baby come from?
It evaporated in my belly;
   turned into a fog
and drifted through my skin.

What a din of hospital trolleys
and cry of squeaky wheels.
The smokes of winter rise
like incense from the tarmac
outside my window.
    A night
has dropped out of my life.
An infant pulled
from between my legs.

I lie like a female Christ —
marks on my wrists, my ankles.

There are two of me now —
the one who gave birth
and the one with a stone baby
calcifying inside.

My body aches and burns;
the bruises talk to me.
I came to – hair and makeup
         fixed in place.
The smell of lambswool
makes me vomit.

The baby at my side is a dummy;
though it moves and wails.

I stroke my sunken belly –
for I feel it growing still;
growing and stretching
inside of me.

MARY STUART

In my end is my beginning

Prologue

With a sharp comb dipped in ink I've tattooed my life story all over my body. I've tattooed the footprints of my children – this way I carry their walking with me; the footprints of my twins who died before their feet touched the ground. And the footprints of my one-year-old son, James, whom I pray for daily.

I
Dent-De-Lion

Because I bore the lion of my father's country
my Maries and I picked dandelions –
          lion's teeth.
All our childhood we picked them –

blowball, cankerwort,
doon-head-clock, witch's gowan,
monk's head, priest's crown, worm rose

Mary Queen of Scots
Mary Queen of Scots

I held their gold beneath my chin;
imagined the lion rampant – its tongue,
its claws on my skin.

When I find the tallest stalk
I know how much I'll grow.

I weave their sun-bells
into my wedding bouquet. When I blow

seeds from the puffball
and three remain –
three children will I bear.

Mary Queen of Scots
Mary Queen of Scots

II
The Caulbearer

When he was born
a shimmer of womb-skin
stretched across his face –
        I knew then
he would always be
with me.

I carried the caul
through all my years in captivity.
I imagined the membrane
attached to his plump baby face
like a coral headdress;

        I spoke to it,
willed it to carry my letters,
my messages into the drowning
depths of his night sleeping head.

III
Daffadowndilly

Despite the westerly gales,
despite the persistence of snowfall
the daffodils are opening.

They are opening
the way tapestries, laboured at
one stitch at a time, suddenly arrive
at something whole.

Mary is stitching her name
over and over, pulling
the threads through
her long fingers.

For nineteen years
her name has been a plaything.
The ends of her fingers weave
puns and anagrams.

She is a woman
of many names –
she has woven a self
to match each name –

Tu te Marieras
Veritas Armata
Sa Vertue M'attire
Tu as Martyre

And the daffodils, they too
have many names –

Daffadowndilly, Narcissus,
Lenten lily, Easter bell.

How they weave themselves
out of the grass, out
of the green shoots
and sheathed leaves;
heads hung, necks
waiting to be snapped.

IV
The Mermaid and the Hare

Though all my life
I've worn dresses of mohair,
damask or serge, stiffened in the neck
       with buckram;

though I wear breeding layers
of petticoats, farthingales
expanded with hoops of whalebone;

they've removed my heart-shaped cap,
my mourning veil, stripped
me bare to the waist,

replaced my silver hose-covered legs
with the wet mucus of a fish tail.

Two husbands dead –
they visit me nightly.
In dreams my hands turn into gudgeons

chubs, loaches; the white magic
of a hare biting at my heels.

V
Snowdrops

When they are ready
they send for her.
There are so many of them –
men who must watch her die.

The snowdrops outside her window
change colour in the sunrise.

She is tired. She has lain awake all night.
She is dressed in black
with a long white veil – a caul
to keep her son close to her.

She counts the pearl acorn buttons
on her satin dress;
she counts the double string of rosary
hanging from her waist.

Her God is ready for her;
his body hangs above her
and she carries his cross
into the great hall.

Pearl queen –
she imagines the hall is filled with pearls
and the pearls are snowdrops.
Into the sheer purity of it she will fall.

She is going into the arms
of her mother.

In blood she came, in blood she will go –
stripped to red petticoat,
red bodice, red sleeves.

She feels herself glowing
in the centre of the hall –
sister to the fireplace;
curls burning around her pale face,
her auburn eyes.

Hunkering for final prayer
she commits herself, kneels to the block;
hot fur, breath, the pounding
heart of her lapdog
pressing against her leg.

She gasps as the phoenix in her chest
breaks apart her body
with two blows –

one from each wing
as it rose.

VI
Red and White

Though it was the colour of mourning,
for my wedding I wanted to wear white –

The colour of fresh snow and milk
The colour of Isis and for wrapping the dead
The colour cloaking the early monks
The colour of the sacrificial lamb
The colour of the transfiguration of our Lord
The colour of the unicorn

My colours are red and white –
a white veil flows from my pale face
and tight red curls.
When I walk in the garden I scatter sunlight.

I am titanium white
I am Sirius
I am an Artic fox
My heart is ermine

I am a white horse ridden by Conquest;
you will remember my name.

BURNING THE STUMP

He made a symbol out of the tree stump.
      Hacked through its roots
(the stringy neck of the woman he hated),
dug a mud ditch around it – black moat
of earth writhing with worms and beetles.
Poured petrol and coal
into the axe-smashed heart of it,
       set it on fire.

The air smouldered and sparked,
flames rising like a spray of daffodils;
the changing sprawl of smoke –
      waves of starlings.

He sat beside it, hair
the colour of scorched wood –
smoke and salt on his skin.

The stump burned inside him
as it burned in our garden
for two days and two nights
like a mini-volcano –
      embers eating into the centre
until it cracked and dissolved;
until the red and black
charred and charcoaled.

All that is left is dead wood
chopped to pieces
      like broken sculptures.
They lie in a heap by our front door –

if I stare at them long enough
I can make out an arm,
          a head, a foot.

Though the stump is gone
the burning clings to him.
He brings it into our house,
turning our bed
into a kind of pyre
on which we die
          all night.

DEGAS' *THE TUB*

for Vicki Feaver

It's the way she lies abandoned,
Jezebel, to her liquid bronze bath; hair
dripping over the lip of the tub,
as if recovering from a marathon
or from giving birth.
Like the post-natal bath I had
in the shock-white hospital –
blood streaking the water,
even the gleaming metal taps.

Her slim body bathes in the shallow
pool – sponge in hand resting against
the edge; hips wide, breasts lolling,
a forearm reaching out
seemingly unconnected to her shoulder.
He has made a map out of her skin –
carved the shapes of countries into her
like scar tissue on the split bark of a tree.

Every time I give birth it's as if my body
is snapped in two, stitched back together
and handed a bundle, another mouth to satisfy.
But she has no such cares;
lost in the waves of her hair,
eyes shut as she absentmindedly holds
her foot. One leg raised, bent across the other,
the straight of her shin following the line
of her outstretched arm, meeting
together in the crux of a triangle.

You simply cannot imagine
that one day soon the dogs
will have her. Leaving only skull,
handbone and foot.

LOT'S WIFE

for Pansy Maurer-Alvarez

I.
Cleopatras – my calla lilies
evoke cobras, milk-bathed skin,
aboriginal queens.
        I planted them
in a blue ceramic pot
outside my bedroom window.

I planted them in darkness,
late August – a last defence
against the shrinking of summer.

I planted them to cup, hold,
preserve the sun's warmth
a little while longer.
        Yellow coiling spathes –
flower-sculptures caught in motion:
opening, unwinding.

The lilies guard my sleeping
like terracotta warriors.
At night the wall between us
dissolves and they enter
my dreams –
        silk-cloaked angels
lifting and carrying me
into the hills.

2.
Every day is the same –
the radio talking to the kitchen walls
and she tending to her herbs.
       She's called them after operas –
Tosca, *La Traviata*, *Aida* and *Carmen* –
lined them up on her windowsill.

This is her home, her life
for as long as she can remember.

Last week she pulled a shallot
       from her garden –
the sole survivor of forty bulbs
planted in the spring.
Held it by its tail like a mouse,
mud dripping from its yellowing head,

sat it on a square napkin,
the outer skin peeling back.
       She rolled its name and variations
round and round in her mouth
like an incantation.

There's a tree stump
in the living room,
it resembles a head –
they use it as a coffee table.
Sometimes she examines
the pale green circles of lichen
for signs – patterns, love letters.
Sometimes they become
the joined up shapes
of her favourite constellations -
the Water Snake, Bird-of-Paradise,
       the Hunting Dog.

This day is different —
even the birds know and are silent.
An empty wine glass on the shelf;
her head, a cloud of sleeplessness
like the dark cloud of tree
that hangs in her neighbour's garden.
      The neighbour they'll be leaving behind
like all the other neighbours on the street —
men and women she's fed
at her table; the children
who grew up with her own.
A sheepskin rug is slung
over the back of a chair;
an untuned piano props up
a photo of her dead mother
holding her two daughters,
while they were still small
enough to hold.

Today she's leaving
all of this behind.
Her husband is on a righteous mission —
he's taking her somewhere new,
he's taking her somewhere beyond the hills.

He thinks she has no regrets.
He thinks she has no one
to look back for.

3.
Worried she was cold
I draped her favourite cloak around her
breathing in the last gasps
of her perfume –
        the sticky scent
of bergamot orange, lemon,
heart of jasmine.

I'm trying to imagine
her face in the featureless pillar
of rock salt that stands
        before me.
I imagine she can hear me.

Where does the heart go
        when it stops?
What does the mouth close on
when the lungs are stilled?

She's standing on a hill
caught between sky and sea;
her cloak billowing.
From a distance
it hangs mid-air like the flower
        of a calla lily
or body of a dust devil –
red and swirling.

THE UN-MOTHER

The clouds of a new dawn whisper around me –
or are they nurses?

The blue firmament is a light-rattled ceiling;
the lighthouse of the doctor shines above me.

My body is a reef – it is growing from me.
I have octopus arms and legs; this bed
cannot contain me.

I am fighting against myself, head wrapped
in a cloud or a clamp of hands.

I yell in an underwater language.

I yell for the baby formed in the lowest
parts of the earth – for the burning ball of flesh
now tearing my skin to strips of tissue paper.

Only there is no baby left.

I am simply a tree making shapes
in the wind – losing parts of myself
to the coming winter.

NIGHT POINSETTIAS

The snow has not yet drowned
in thunder, lightning, or in rain.

The snow has not yet drowned
the garden completely.

The house is bat-black, air still,
bedroom doors unopened.

Small breathing rises in each room –
my daughter, my son

asleep among butterfly wings,
blue stars, waning moons.

Ice-animals creep across the window –
see how their footprints leave

thousands of spilt needles
pricking the dark at every turn.

On nights like these only the fresh blood
of my three poinsettias can be heard –

when shall we three meet again
in thunder, lightning, or in rain?

REDWOOD AVENUE II: SIERRA REDWOODS

Wind plays the Sierra
Redwood xylophone.

I know your height,
the breadth of your bones

but how far under my feet
do you go?

Digging your root-heels
into the centre of the earth.

MADAME ECOSSE

With a smash and razzmatazz, flyers and cavalcades,
Madame Ecosse was born. Politicised

'doon the watter'
singing along to *The Road to the Isles,*

"this is my country." Madame Ecosse,
lionised, trail-blazer, "Stop the world,

Scotland wants to get on"
with loudspeakers and song.

Not a snowball's chance in hell,
they said; but Madame Ecosse, you wooed us –

18,397 of us to be exact. Winifred Margaret Ewing,
Scottish National Party.

A turn up for the books to the soundtrack
of 'We want Winnie'. Woman of the moment,

galvanising the tartan express. Raising a storm,
letting loose electric shivers.

Enemy of the state, thorn in the flesh,
mad woman, maenad, baiter of people.

"Where you been and why you went?" –
the words of a three-year-old, your son.

"Father will have to be mother
when I'm in the heart of Westminster".

Then for 24 years Brussels heard
Scotland! Scotland! Scotland!

In the end you went back to the beginning,
Madame Ecosse; the immortal words said —

The Scottish Parliament, adjourned in 1707
is hereby reconvened.

WOMEN OF TRIDENT: POEM FOR THREE VOICES

A storm in the heart and a fire in the brain; a clamour of furies
– Aeschylus

First voice:
They move with great purpose – steel whales
sliding up the Narrows, sun firing
off their silver backs. How they shine –
white lighting burning up dull waves.

Second voice:
Six gulls, six white chests,
grey wings folded, red stick-legs.
They edge closer, closer to me
until they touch my shadow –
dark twin.
   Red beaks,
red webbed feet.
How bright everything is –
staunch sunrays flood the ground.
Gulls caw at me,
their needle mouths shut
then open.

Third voice:
I am wrapped up like a doll
in a cowl of Aran wool –
warm creamy animal
curling around my neck.

And now I am knitting a boom,
a web to catch the teardrop hulls
of submarines, black holes
oozing up the Clyde; nurturing the seeds
of a dozen suns in their bellies.

I will tie it to the Gantocks.
I will stretch it across the Firth
to the Cloch Lighthouse.

Watch the sleek bodies coming in now –
see them corral, one by one,
in my net:

All voices:
Victorious, Vigilant,
Vanguard, Vengeance
          is mine.

First voice:
I collect footprints, hand prints,
paw prints. I collect the movements
of waves. I make sculptures
out of twigs, leaves
and sail them down the river.

Second voice:
I come to the Clyde and stare.

Like the yellow tide marker
I measure how high the waters rise.

I stand here, stalwart, day and night.
I have an affinity with the waves.

Here am I, one among so many;
I appear and disappear, transform,

rise and fall with great frequency.
I roll onwards to the shore then slide

back into myself. My roots, my memories
are buried in this beach. I have lived here

all my life: the Clyde pours from me
and everything within its depths

are a part of me.

First voice:
I have learned to live with them;
my body has become attuned
to them.
       My blood thickens,
my limbs ache when they propel
through the deep veins of the Clyde.

My head splits with their sonar calls,
the hollow ringing follows me
like a shadow on the brain.

Third voice:
There's a pool of light, a sun-spell, on the river.
A full-rigged frigate rises out of it suddenly.

I bring my baby to the Firth daily,
lower the pram hood to flush his cheeks
with seaweed-smirr.

I wheel him beside the river in his pushchair
until he finds sleep. Then I link arms with the air
and name the dark visions as they slide
by my left side.

All voices:
Victorious, Vigilant,
Vanguard, Vengeance
          is mine.

First voice:
I bring my children's drawings
to the Coal Pier and toss them
onto the back of the Clyde.

I scatter their baby clothes, toys
and trinkets, their first tooth,
hairs cut from their heads.

Third voice:
There is so much one can do in four minutes –
four minutes to lift my boy from his pram,
cup his eggshell fontanels,
stroke his liquid blonde curls.
Four minutes to undress him, soothe him,
settle him to my chest.

41

Shadow of pram, shadow of hands,
mother of rivers.
The tide is rising; the waters reach me.
The ship has gone, the fish —
they touch me.

Here come the crows —
two of them and then three,
heads bobbing among the dry,
crackly, fired-up seaweed.

Second voice:
Clouds, clouds, bodies
on black benches surround this bay.
The Clyde creates pools on the shingle,
the hills dip at my back.
Everything is moving around me,
the skeletons of old ships unsettle me.
The band of bladder wrack on the beach
is my loosened hair.

I birth jellyfish.
I have a vision of shadows
with no bodies to cast them.
I shall be blast
to a silhouette etched in stone.

With my body
I shall turn this beach
into a work of art.

First voice:
I move with great purpose among steel whales.
I flag up their every departure, arrival.
I speak in the low frequency
of a woman in prayer.

The Clyde knows how many
and whose deaths she carries
starlit to my shore.

All voices:
Victorious, Vigilant,
Vanguard, Vengeance
          is mine.

NIGHT CROSSING

The ferry hums through unseen waves;
strip lighting flickering above our heads,
late night conversations struggle around us.
The streetlights of Gourock grow smaller.
Squinting, I transform the orange balls
into rows of glowing crosses,
Calvaries, ascending the black hillside.

I've been here before, many times –
my sixteenth birthday
when he proposed on the upper deck
in the heart of this dark estuary
against the backdrop of Orion
and the Seven Sisters.
The land-lights are drifting further
away as we sail deeper into the Firth;
life swarming beneath us –
basking sharks, mackerels, silver eels,
a colony of flame shells, sewing themselves
together on the seabed.

We skim across the surface of the Clyde,
across dark waves and into dark skies.
I imagine my mother's final crossing
strapped to the ambulance bed, breathing
through an oxygen mask, like a struggling
high altitude climber or deep sea diver.
The streetlights form signals now,
signs from dry land, the intermittent blip
of car lights, journeying the shoreline –
a sort of Morse code, message
from the other side.

DEATH OF A SNOWMAN

All night the great ball of snow
disturbs my dreams;
               all night
it floats into the sky of my mind
transforming into torso, hip bone
and thigh. A great shadow
in the middle of the fish-glitter lawn –
his back to the living room window.

Moribund snowman –
I put you together with my very own hands;
rolled you from the ground,
watched you grow until I could push you
through the grass no longer.

First it was for the sheer pleasure –
I patted snow in my hands like wet sand,
closing my fist, cupping it
into a hard, compact ball –
a perfect sphere.

I could feel it humming
in harmony with the internal music
of my body.
              Then I rolled it
through the garden marvelling
as snow molecules gathered
and grew beneath my wringing skin.

I rolled him between my fingers.
I rolled him into a full moon.
I gave him a name,
I gave him eyes, a nose, a mouth.
I made him the keeper of my garden.

What does it mean to be encased in the elements;
to be at once something and nothing?

I formed him in the garden.
I gave him eight faces;
pressed shut his plum lips,
rubbed off the tip of his ear
to resemble a Nigerian funeral statue.

There are bird tracks on his shoulder;
his bulging eyes, his crumpled nose.
If he were a woman
he would break apart daily.

Every day he is different –
today he has a human head and a beak;
cowrie shell eyes, and a gaping mouth hole.
I make him a butterfly mask
to usher in the spring.
       I paint a picture of him
to bury in the ground
when he is gone.

The birds peck at him.
They land on his head, his shoulder, his toes.
Were I to marry a man like that –
a blizzard of a man, weather-bound,
buttoned-up and stony-eyed;
carrot-nosed and stony-mouthed.

The earth will swallow him up —
the earth will reveal her grasses and eat him.
Already the garden is hatching her plan.

DAPHNE AND THE SITKA SPRUCE

The storm-felled spruce came to me
fresh and bloody in the rain,
          a severed leg.
Such rawness, as if a dozen hearts
were pounding out of the log.
I thought of the last witch
burned for growing horse's hooves
out of her daughter's hands and feet.

The spruce bark peeled off in circles,
exposing the fire and ochre
of the inner ligaments of the tree.
I saw the body of Jenny Horne
fastened to the log with an iron chain,
crows in her eyes, tar-smeared skin.

My hands grew white spots of lichen,
moss crawled in between my fingers.
I couldn't speak, my spine stiffened,
straightened, the storm-spruce grew
up my back until all I could do
was lie down across the path.

Will they fashion me
into a piano soundboard – converting
string vibrations into deep timbre tones?
Or will they carve out of me
a stake to be driven into the ground
against which the bodies of women
will be transformed?

DINNER

I am a crucifix
strapped to a table.
I can feel the baby coming –
its body pushing between my tied legs.

The doctor will come
when he's good and ready

But the fish in my belly is slipping,
slipping away from me.
It thinks it's an autumn leaf –
crushed and falling
from a tree.

I am that tree.
Rooted in red leaves –
I've been here so long algae
is growing around me;
its green webbing stretched
across my face.

My baby is blackening
in the tunnel of my body;
it's leaking from me
into a puddle of leaves.

The doctor does not come –
he is still eating;
      cutting, forking,
savouring his rare meat.

THE SPOON CARVER'S WIFE

In the belly of his shed he carves
mysteries, ancient alphabets,
into wooden spoons.
Sits on a stump, knife in hand,
slicing into birch, elm, sycamore, ash;
slicing them into long, thin tongues.
He sits in the centre of the open red doors
carving the faces of everyone he knows
into spoons – he has a feel for the shape
of their skulls, translates them
into wood and locks them up nightly.

His spoons are perfect specimens –
steel-carved smooth, shaped, rounded –
the bowl, handle, crank and keel –
then held up to the test of a light bulb.
He is slicing the days away –
every curl of bark peeled off
as he trims, thins, cross-cuts, chips
next to a mountain of chopped wood.
Even asleep in our bed, his hands mimic
the knife's action. When I enrage him
he punishes the spoon of my likeness.

He keeps our children's spoons
with him always – carries them
around in his pocket.
He's trying to keep them safe
from wild animals, decay, from cracking
and splitting, from the inevitable fires.
I am turning in his hand – he's paring

away at me too; paring me to the bone.
Our children are stick children,
I – a stick woman. One day
he'll cut me clean through.

APPLE TREES

She's planting apple trees in the garden,
one for each of her children.

She digs holes for the young saplings —
slicing through the earth,

through wireworm and click beetle;
heaving shovelful after shovelful

of soil onto a blue tarpaulin.
With her bare hands she pans

the mud for stones. Digs
up rocks, fist-sized, builds

a cairn out of them, a sort of totem,
at the bottom of the garden.

And when she's dug deep enough,
carefully sits the young trees in place;

tamps their roots, fills the holes up
adding water and a layer of mulch.

At night she feels them growing
the way she feels her children's bones

lengthening in their sleep.
From the moonlit window

overlooking the garden,
she can feel the roots unfurling,

stretching towards her
under the earth.

HEARTBEAT

The Firth is as calm as the waters
that no longer fill my belly;
clouds – pale as my blood-drained,
        child-drained skin.
They pierced me with a witch's nail;
they unplugged me.

I want to sink into the Clyde –
sink into its amniotic fluids.
The doctors and nurses rise out of my feet
like the hills of Gourock –
solid and unmoving.

The faint crescent of a daylight moon
is my baby's heartbeat –
a half heart stilled in the sky,
unreachable.
                It hovers above us all –
above my Firth of Clyde belly,
above the surgical hills,
above the whole earth
like Dali's Christ.

I want to push the moon back inside
of me and let it grow
and grow whole, round and full.

Then I want to feel it fall
from between my legs; hold it
        fresh and sticky,
beating between my breasts.

BIRTHING A WATERFALL

I have dreams of being buried alive.
My head's so heavy
I can barely lift it from the bed.

They said I birthed my baby
but how can I be sure?

They bandaged my head
up like a mummy
with thick white gauze.

I heard howls from behind closed doors
off the long white corridor.
They've wheeled me into a zoo of wolves.

      They left me alone
in a metal cribbed bed,
trapped on my back – wrists and ankles
leather-strapped and tied apart.

I arched with every white hot
tightening steaming through
my body.

I fell into dreams of flooding
and of pushing a red pram
through a river.

Then I gave birth to a waterfall –
I heard its watery cries
through my bandaged hood.

And I birthed again, this time
to silence and blackness
which seemed without end.

SHE LAY DOWN DEEP BENEATH THE SEA: MEDITATIONS ON DUNOON'S VICTORIAN PIER

I.
I am bound, rooted, salt-stung,
tree-limbed, iron bolted.
I live with my memories –
echoes of footsteps arriving,
departing; ghost boats
      at my thighs.

Every timber part of me swims
with zooplankton. My only neighbour
is my reflection. The sky
is sailing around me.
Fenders of rock elm protect me.
My mouth is a softwood deck
      of pitch pine.

I've been here so long
living out my days in this estuary.
I am locked in a blue room –
the summers of my childhood
pressing down on my skin;
I am up to my neck in tide.

2.

The pier is a series of joined-at-the-hip bodies.
The pier is a timber tongue flying out of the Firth.
The pier is a woman on her back; fog-clouds –
bed-sheets, pulled up over her head.
When the pier opens her legs –
it's a window to nowhere.
The pier drags her bladder-wrack
and dabber-lock body through spirals
of underwater currents.
When the tide falls the pier floats ashore
like a battered toy.
The pier is breaking apart.
Her legs are a row of piano keys
playing in A minor.
The pier is sun-aged and storm-scarred;
she has seen many departures.
The pier is an arch of hysteria
holding her secrets deep in the very girders.
The pier is tired – looking always across the Firth.
She sits in the shallows, among rocks,
her back bare – tubular spine, a hint of ribs.
She remembers the names of her steamers:
Meg Merrilies, Jeanie Deans, Heather Bell.
At the end of her life
the pier has leapt off of herself
and is simply floating in the water.

3.
We will always return to the pier –
she is our end point, our home.
Grey seals and bone whales
sing songs of her water logs,
salty in the brazen sun.
No steamer comes to her now.
The shoreline is carved with the facade
of her wooden sisters –
the remnants of cast-off piers.
She is half-dressed in a shock of fronds
and bladders; she is barnacle-legged
       and limpet-cheeked.
She is our night constellation on the Firth;
       our lifeline and lifetime satellite.

4.
At the Opening of the New Pier, 1898.
She absorbs the sounds of the rabble
down to the very core of her timber bones.
Their voices preserved in the lichen
and limpet shells beginning their slow journey
of attachment around her plump new legs.
Voices to be held to the ears of children,
years after those voices have stilled.
You, on this new pier can never leave,
fade, never age, enter war. You
in the Glengarry bonnet, flat cap,
top hat, bowler, ribboned straw hat
present at the birth of a pier under bunting
and flag poles have become her story.
Abandoned woman of pleasure, daughter
of stillness – the end that comes to us all;
where are your people now?

POLPHAIL VILLAGE

I have long had this premonition
of a bright day and a deserted house.
– Anna Akhmatova

Only the bodies of birds, bats and sheep
inhabit this place

so when we come here, we become bird-like,
bat-like, sheep-like.

Everything is transformed –
washing machine drums have become eyes;

a cairn of stones – a small body
curled in the corner of a muddy couch.

We taste brick dust, wet fur, sea air
on our tongues.

It's the first day of New Year
and somehow my body feels as unlived-in

and crumbling as the houses
breaking around us.

How they speak to us – the door
hanging off its hinges; the emerald

puddle of algae in the bathtub;
glass shattering under our boots.

A flight of stairs step off mid-air
to somewhere we cannot follow.

Here, walls sprout words, pictures,
the enormous face of a woman –

her gold-touched eyes watching
from a distance.

The hardened spines of winter gorse
are closing in, the tarmacked ground fractured;

its cracks matching the heart line,
head line and life line on my left hand.

We walk through the Polphail inside of us –
smashed up houses, writing on the wall.

They call it a ghost village
but there are no ghosts here, simply

another expression of ourselves.

SIGNS

There were three of them:
a dead magpie, a live toad,
and the autumn equinox.

It was as if the garden was trying
to tell me something.

I couldn't bear
to go near the magpie.
       For days, they came down
from the trees in droves
clicking at the smashed body.

After you buried it
       a scatter of black
and white feathers
formed themselves into letters.

The toad sat poised
on the grass –
a brown speckled stone.

We walked around it, examining
       from every angle.
The children shouted –
threw leaves to make it flinch.

I ran for my camera
and crouched in front
of its crab stance – snapping
the horizontal amber lines
       of its pupils.

I could almost see into the jewel
in its skull – the toadstone.

In the midst of all this –
the equinoxium
       passed unnoticed

like the middle distance
between the cradle
       and the grave.

REDWOOD AVENUE III: CROSSING

Walking your avenue
is like crossing the Red Sea –

each height-hungry tree
holds back a full force tide.

I mouth your names
as if they are the names of God:

Wawona, Toos-pung-ish, Hea-mi-withic

SEPTEMBER IS NOT THE BIRTH OF THINGS

September is a stripped trunk of bay laurel,
a valley of rhubarb wands, sky
reflecting the shale rocks
            with layered tongues –
quartz clouds breaking through slate.

September is a haul of brambles
rotting on a claw
of branches, pulp of bracken fronds
browning at the edges,
crimson wings of fuchsia –
dripping Chinese lanterns.

September is not the birth of things
though it was the month
she was born in.
            The month
when evergreens become
the muscle of the wind's song.
The month they turn
into a pack of howling dogs –
        birth pangs of winter
in the chill dawn.

That September I huddled
in my room – for three long weeks
not another soul came near.
My heart leapt into my mouth
when she slipped out
            quiet as a doll.

Then her call rang through me –
collared doves
in the grey September air.

MAGPIES

The tree outside my window
is wild with Pica pica —

dozens of them sitting there
like papier-mâché birds —
the set square lines of their backs,
beaks raised to a midday sky.
      A sky which doesn't know
what to make of the bleached
wing-tips or the blind coal heads.

They say the tongue of a magpie
contains a drop of blood
from the devil.
      If you bit my tongue
what do you think would happen?

I'm watching them
through the window
sitting on the large leafless,
twiggy tree — a maze of dark veins.
      The tree is a kind of Medusa
rooted to the earth, unable to claw
the charm of magpies out of her hair.

      Sometimes you watch me
the way I'm watching these corvids
as one by one they disappear
leaving behind a small body of them;

and I not knowing if they number
eight for heaven
        or nine for hell.

CAR CRASH

Under the star-lights
of the operating room –
under Sirius, the Seven Sisters
and Orion's Belt; metal hands slide
into my body's red canal.
I'm swimming in a black lagoon.
They have my baby by the head
and pulling. Someone
climbs on top of me,
pushes on my belly, punching
my baby downwards;
fists like rocks.
With scissors shiny as sparklers
they cut me. I think of flowers –
roses, poppies, dahlias.
The waves of Tiree flow in
on beaches above my head.
He reaches into my uterus,
pulls out my limp baby
then sews me up into a virgin again.
Hours later they give him to me;
his head, dented, like a crashed car.

SHADOWS

I didn't know
but I was preparing
for your leaving.

You who have been
growing outside of my womb
        for five years now.

I've been seeing
embryos everywhere –
the mummified crocodile
        at the museum
lying under glass
like a tiny branch
of carved walnut wood –

It looks as if it's sleeping,
it looks as if it's been cut
from its mother's belly.

It's nearly time to open the locks,
loosen our pleats,
unravel the knots,
untie the laces in our shoes –
this is another kind of birth
and separation.

I've been digging up your footprints,
planting them in a pot.
I've been giving the birds your hair
to build their nests with.

I didn't know it
but I've been preparing
for your leaving for some time now —
practicing watching the gulls
fly away from behind
my closed eyes.

The midsummer sun
has turned the garden to water.
A solitary bee dreams
from flower to flower
       on my dress.

As our shadows start to shorten,
you'll no longer leap in mine
all day
       like a hungry fish;
and my shadow
will have to re-learn
what else
       it exists for.

THE OWL GIRL

My daughter
sleeps every night gripping
the crumpled picture of a barn owl
and every night I tip-toe in
to the pink flush of her room
and release it
      from her fingers.

At the bird zoo
I was caught in the orange irises
of an eagle owl –
it held me in the sunset rings
of its eyes.
      But it was the skulls
in the keeper's timber hut
that drew me:

the skull of a badger,
two of mountain hare.
Their fused flat bones,
open hole of snout, teeth gaps
in the jaw.
      Eye holes, ear holes,
holes for the soul
to leak through.

They became the skulls
of my children –
their soft fontanels
pulsing under my fingers.

At night,
when I slip into her room,
I place the heart-shaped owl face
under her pillow
to fly.

BIRTH MOTHER

No woman knows what her womb bears
(Exile of the sons of Uisliu)

1.

White flutter of minor falls —
stone gobs dribble spittle
into the water hole.

Wet rocks red,
chuckies and pebbles too.
The pool pulls eyes
towards its shallow
bowl —

a strange auburn burn
caught in a fairy ring.
What life will it bring?

What life?
      Nobody knows.

2.

The shock of the sudden pull,
the pull, the pull —
the weight of millstones

or an angry bull
sewn into my belly.
Imagine your baby

said a voice, a voice
from the bottom of a well.
Imagine her head

on the bed, on the bed.
My body burning,
fire cracking,

on the verge
of popping, sucking
gulps of sweet gas,

a morass.
Dizzily charged –
the animal is thrusting

its way into the hell
of a noise. Then a silence
so loud it's...

LINDOW MAN

They keep you in a dark corner
and at first the voyeur in me
is thrilled to see the peat-preserved
      flesh, bone, hair.

      But when I look at you
I'm surprised by my desire
to touch your cheek, stroke
the delicate scroll
      of your ear –
head turned to the side,
chin to chest
as if resting in sleep.

I want to give you back
into the arms of the bog.
      But they keep you here,
freeze-dried, in a glass cage.

Lying on a bracken-brown bed –
      your curled up body;
skin tanned to leather;
centuries of peat
dyeing your hair red.
      I know your last meal
was charred bread
and somehow mistletoe.

If these glass walls could –
they would smash and release you
      into the air.

If the dried quag under you could –
it would open up and swallow you
          back into the earth.

HOW TEMPORARY THE SNOW IS

Before Numa Pompilius, agent of the gods, gave January and February their names,
the days between December and March had no name – they were a no man's land of days.
Now, on the Ides of January, I long for these days not to exist by name or on paper
but to roll one into another like a never ending snowstorm.

The snow creates its own light.
When I opened the curtains
the sky was snow and darkened ivory
and you, behind me, a shadow
on the bed.
       Only three things
could I think about: the whiteness
bearing down on the window;
your silhouette stretched out on the bed;
and the taste of the fridge in my mouth.

All night the snow fell.
I woke to a snow playground –
the trees had turned into polar animals.
The bed sheets – a tangle of winter
unravelled around me.

The snow lay heavy on me all night
but when I woke was powder-light,
drifting through the air.

I've taken to sitting by the bay window
overlooking the snow-wracked garden.
The fire is burning itself out in the fireplace;
my blood thickening as the snow falls.

Since you left I've forgotten how to speak.
Every deafening creak in this house
is my language now.
        The tiniest crack in the door
lets in slugs nightly – their soft bodies
shrugging across the wall.

Since you left I've become
a mute white statue –
a kind of snowwoman.

Tonight I went down to the river –
the Clyde Firth rushing up
the stone shingle in darkness.
The air – a smother of darts
flying towards me; sleety snow
white as milk teeth converges to rain.

Because like the snow you left.
Because you can never stay.
Because the garden cannot hold you.

Only three things could I think about...

POEM FOR A GARDEN

Prologue

And what do the smash of rhododendrons know?
A squall of them spilling over the wall –
sun driving its heat through the head
of each flower; a growing shudder
rusting on the ground below –
pink stars crumbling on the pavement.

I.
It was the height of summer
and the sun stopped in the head of a bull.

The garden wailing with flowers,
shorn grasses writhing,
birds sniping in the deciduous leaves,
the Clyde breeze sifting through the town.

It was the height of summer
        and the constant light
hurt my eyes, hurt the green poinsettia
on the windowsill.

Then the light hurt everything –
the birds stopped, the shorn grass
stilled, the breeze changed
direction.
        All became as the poinsettia,
all dreamed of the darkness,
of our real red selves.

2.
At Glengyle – listen
to the street-cats yowl.

The collared doves' cooing
crawls through the air
with the cries of tired children.

And the wood pile groans –
listen to the rings
of the cut stump moan.

Look to the Rosemary
in the Belfast sink;
look to the bay tree

and to the hand prints
of the rhubarb leaves,
the climbing rose,

and under the gooseberry
where my babies grow.

3.
The rhubarb in the garden hounds me –
its thick pink stalks rising out of the ground
the mound of it grows bigger by the day –
no one will pick it, cook it. Soon it
will suffocate the garden entirely –
its huge flag leaves bend towards me.
I watch it from the window –
wild animal – I hear its music
when the wind blows – a sort of jungle fever –
there is no peace when the rhubarb grows.

4.
Trinities of strawberries.
Brute-red – the little knuckles hang
angry as thunder.

What a wonder they are –
salvaging themselves
every summer without fail
from the bottom of the rotten
green sacks stacked
at the back of the garden.

Strawberries to die for –
sun-bells, green speckled skins
growing beside the red –
like the wheat and the chaff:

one shall be picked for the right
and one shall be picked for the left.

5.
Deadheaded fuchsia flowers,
        like birds feet
and red as war paint,
scattered on the ground.

6.
I walk the circumference of my garden
through long grass and ditch – I stride
past apple trees, cherry saplings, a silver birch,
the pins and thrums of late primroses;
        grappling for room.

Where do the grasses go?
They burn, they burn.
Where do the dandelion puffs blow?
They catch on my tongue,
seed in the air,
bloom in my womb,
grow on my thumb.

It was the height of summer
and the sun stopped in the head of a bull.

ICELAND POPPIES

the women, they do not wait until they are very old for death to take them,
but…take themselves out of life, some by means of the poppy.
– Heracleides

I've been growing them in my garden
for some time now.
And what a row of glories they are –
fire-flowers pulsing in the grass.

When the sun catches their gold
and orange backs, they glow
like stained glass – their papery skins
mirroring my own.

I'm trying to imagine the warm petals
melting on my tongue,
sticking to the roof of my mouth
like communion wafers.
And then biting down
on the raw green seeds.

When the time comes
I want it to be spring.
I want to make my bed
among the poppies –
for the sun to shine through me
as through a cathedral window;

to dissolve
on tongues of air.

NOTES

'Twilight Sleep'
Developed in the early 19th Century, Twilight Sleep was
a drug which combined pain relief with amnesia so that
women could give birth while conscious and yet entirely
forget the experience.

'She Lay Down Deep Beneath the Sea'
Title from a drawing by Tracey Emin.

ACKNOWLEDGEMENTS

Many of these poems, or versions of them, first appeared in *Poetry* (Chicago), *The Manchester Review, Critical Survey Journal, The Atlanta Review, Raum, Paris Lit Up*; and online *at BODY, Transmission, And Other Poems Blog, The Ofi Press* (Mexico), *Ink, Sweat & Tears, The Lake, Spotlight,* and *Glasgow Review of Books*. A selection of these poems were published in the anthology *Our Real Red Selves* (Vagabond Voices, 2015).

I would like to acknowledge Tina Cassidy's *Birth: The Surprising History of how we are Born* (Grove Press, 2007) as a useful resource for many of the birth poems. I would like to thank the Scottish Book Trust and Vicki Feaver for the mentoring opportunity I received as part of the New Writers Award Scheme. The wonderful nine months of mentoring I had with Vicki Feaver made this book possible. I would also like to acknowledge the work of Pascale Petit and Sujata Bhatt whose poetry in particular has been a constant source of inspiration.

Thanks to Tariq Latif for proof reading the collection and for his valuable input into many of the poems, thanks also to Gillian Prew and Nikki Magennis for their help in honing these poems. I'd like to especially thank Fiona Frank for her generosity in allowing me to use her aunt, Hannah Frank's, wonderful drawing as the cover of this collection. And special thanks to Edwin Smet for his wonderful work on the design of this book; Kelly Davio for her hard work and diligence in bringing the book together; and most of all to Todd Swift and Eyewear Publishing for generously supporting and believing in my work.

EYEWEAR PUBLISHING

EYEWEAR'S TITLES INCLUDE

EYEWEAR
POETRY

KATE NOAKES CAPE TOWN
SIMON JARVIS EIGHTEEN POEMS
ELSPETH SMITH DANGEROUS CAKES
CALEB KLACES BOTTLED AIR
GEORGE ELLIOTT CLARKE ILLICIT SONNETS
HANS VAN DE WAARSENBURG THE PAST IS NEVER DEAD
BARBARA MARSH TO THE BONEYARD
DON SHARE UNION
SHEILA HILLIER HOTEL MOONMILK
MARION MCCREADY TREE LANGUAGE
SJ FOWLER THE ROTTWEILER'S GUIDE TO THE DOG OWNER
AGNIESZKA STUDZINSKA WHAT THINGS ARE
JEMMA BORG THE ILLUMINATED WORLD
KEIRAN GODDARD FOR THE CHORUS
COLETTE SENSIER SKINLESS
ANDREW SHIELDS THOMAS HARDY LISTENS TO LOUIS ARMSTRONG
JAN OWEN THE OFFHAND ANGEL
A.K. BLAKEMORE HUMBERT SUMMER
SEAN SINGER HONEY & SMOKE
HESTER KNIBBE HUNGERPOTS
MEL PRYOR SMALL NUCLEAR FAMILY
ELSPETH SMITH KEEPING BUSY
TONY CHAN FOUR POINTS FOURTEEN LINES
MARIA APICHELLA PSALMODY
TERESE SVOBODA PROFESSOR HARRIMAN'S STEAM AIR-SHIP
ALICE ANDERSON THE WATERMARK
BEN PARKER THE AMAZING LOST MAN
MANDY KAHN MATH, HEAVEN, TIME
ISABEL ROGERS DON'T ASK
REBECCA GAYLE HOWELL AMERICAN PURGATORY
MARION MCCREADY MADAME ECOSSE
MARIELA GRIFFOR DECLASSIFIED
MARK YAKICH THE DANGEROUS BOOK OF POETRY FOR PLANES
HASSAN MELEHY A MODEST APOCALYPSE

EYEWEAR
LITERARY
CRITICISM

MARK FORD THIS DIALOGUE OF ONE - WINNER OF THE 2015 PEGASUS
AWARD FOR POETRY CRITICISM FROM THE POETRY FOUNDATION
(CHICAGO, USA).